1

1 Introduction

Understanding trade developments is a central issue for policy institutions as well as for the private sector since trade dynamics are important determinants of output growth and inflationary pressures coming from import prices. Having a model to infer current trade figures and future trade developments, conditional on macroeconomic scenarios, is important both for policy institutions, which form policy decisions, and for the private sector, which form investment decisions.

There are two main approaches to forecasting trade: large structural macro models and time series models. Large structural models (e.g., Hervé, Pain, Richardson, Sédillot, and Beffy, 2011; Riad, Errico, Henn, Saborowski, Saito, and Turunen, 2012) aim at understanding the economic mechanisms that generate trade dynamics, rather than at achieving the best possible forecasting performance. By contrast, time series models (e.g., Keck, Raubold, and Truppia, 2009; Jakaitiene and Dées, 2012; Yu, Wang, and Lai, 2008; Lin and Xia, 2009) aim at building trade models with good forecasting properties.

Our work belongs in the time series model literature, proposing a dynamic factor model that shows that exploiting the co-movement between macroeconomic variables and trade variables is essential for obtaining accurate short-term forecast of trade variables. We use this model to infer future developments of trade variables given scenarios for macroeconomic variables and to quantify the effect on euro area trade variables of changed macroeconomic conditions in euro area trading partners.

In recent years, factor models have become a workhorse at central banks and international organizations for short-term forecasting of macroeconomic variables. The seminal paper of Giannone, Reichlin, and Small (2008) shows that factor models can handle easily a "ragged edge" data structure, and that they produce very accurate short-term forecasts for U.S. real GDP. Several papers applied the same methodology for short-term forecasting of GDP, inflation, employment, etc., for several countries; for a survey see Bańbura, Giannone, and Reichlin (2011); Bańbura, Giannone, Modugno, and Reichlin (2013). In this paper, we make use of a factor model estimated with the methodology proposed in Bańbura and Modugno (2014): they propose a maximum likelihood estimation methodology based on a modification of the expectation maximization (EM) algorithm that allows to exploit datasets characterized by arbitrary patterns of missing data. Moreover, when using a maximum likelihood estimation approach, it is straightforward to introduce restrictions on the parameters. This approach also allows to identify the nature of the unobserved factors.

We evaluate the model in a pseudo short-term out-of-sample simulation from January

2

2006 to April 2013: at each point in time we generate forecasts, we replicate the data availability as it was at that point in time, but we do not consider data revisions, given the scarce availability of real-time data. We show that a factor model estimated on a panel of trade and macroeconomic data delivers accurate forecasts because it can fully exploit the co-movement in the panel and the earlier releases of the macroeconomic variables. The inclusion of real macroeconomic variables, confidence indicators and prices improves the forecast accuracy over a model that exploits only trade information.[1]

We also find, in contrast to Burgert and Dées (2009), but in line with Marcellino, Stock, and Watson (2003) for other euro area macroeconomic variables, that the "bottom-up" forecast approach for euro area exports and imports delivers forecasts as good as those obtained with a "direct" approach. This result is important, because it allows us to disentangle the contribution to the extra euro-area forecast from different world regions.

We also run a natural experiment and generate the dynamics of trade variables during the great recession conditional on the realized path of macroeconomic variables. Results show that trade developments are well tracked: these results makes our model a suitable tool for conditional scenario analyses.

Finally, factor identification allows us to quantify the effect of an external demand shock from specific regions to extra euro area trade: we use a generalized impulse response function, i.e. the difference between a forecast conditional on an increase in external demand and the correspondent unconditional forecast, and find that a demand shock in BRIC countries has the highest effect on extra-euro area trade.

The paper is organized as follows: section 2 describes the data and trade aggregation. Section 3 describes the model. Section 4 shows the forecasting results, while section 5 shows the conditional forecast exercises. Section 6 concludes.

2 Data

In this paper, we aim at forecasting monthly intra and extra euro area import and export prices and volumes, vis-à-vis euro-area partners: Brazil, Russia, India, China, Japan, South Korea, Switzerland, Denmark, Sweden, the U.K., Turkey, the U.S., Canada, OPEC, and a residual called Rest of the World. There are in total 68 trade data series (import and export volumes and prices from 14 countries plus extra euro area, intra euro area and the Rest of

---

[1]For a discussion of the importance of the timing of data releases in nowcasting within the framework of a factor model, see Bańbura, Giannone, and Reichlin (2011).

the World series). These data are produced by the statistics department of the European Central Bank (ECB).[2]

In addition, for trade data, we exploit the predictive power of 30 macroeconomic variables selected on the basis of their availability: industrial production (IP) in manufacturing (from the euro area, Brazil, Canada, Denmark, the U.K., India, Korea, Russia, Sweden, Turkey and the U.S.); purchasing manager indexes (PMI) of new export orders (euro area, China, the U.K., India, Japan, Korea, Russia, Turkey and the United States); producer price indexes (PPI) in manufacturing (Brazil, Canada, Switzerland, Denmark, India, Japan, Korea, Russia, Sweden and United States), consumer price indexes (CPI) and (PPI) in the euro area; the real effective exchange rate of the euro area, deflated by CPI, vis-à-vis 40 trading partners;[3] and the unemployment rate and retail sales in the euro area. The sample covers monthly observations from January 1995 to April 2013.[4] The dataset is highly unbalanced due to the different publication lag of trade data, with various trading partners (some bilateral data are available before the aggregate), and macroeconomic data. There are also missing observations due to the initial date at which various macroeconomic variables become available.

Figure 1 shows the monthly growth rates of the trade variables used in the paper: export prices, import prices, export volumes, and import volumes. The common feature of these data is the low persistence; in addition, volumes show higher volatility than prices.

Table 1 describes some baseline statistics: mean; standard deviation; absolute value of the autocorrelation coefficient, which is a measure of persistence; and the R^2, computed with a simple autoregressive model of order 1, which is a measure of predictability.

- **Mean** - On average, over the sample, month-on-month (MoM) extra and intra euro area export price inflations both stand at 0.18, while extra and intra euro area import price inflations are slightly higher 0.29 and 0.21, respectively. Imports from Korea show negative price growth. Export volume growth, on average across the sample and across the fourteen countries, is 0.42. High growth is recorded in Russia, China, and Brazil at 0.96, 0.82, and 0.70, respectively. Extra euro area export growth is higher than intra euro area export growth, 0.36 vs 0.19. The average growth in export volumes across the fourteen countries is higher than that in import volumes (0.21). Imports

---

[2]Volume data are available from the ECB's website at the ECB Statistical Data Warehouse, External Trade, under code TRD.M.I6.Y.M.TTT.?.4.VOX; price data are derived as implicit deflators from the corresponding value data.

[3]Code EXR.M.Z65.EUR.ERC0. A at the ECB Statistical Data Warehouse, Exchange Rates.

[4]The data were downloaded on July 31, 2013.

from Japan, the U.K., Canada and OPEC show a negative sign.

- **Standard Deviation** - Volumes display high volatility when compared with prices. Volatility is, on average, 5.35 and 5.43 for export and import volumes, respectively. Changes in price movements have instead more contained fluctuations; the average volatility is 1.46 and 2.17 for export and import prices inflation, respectively.

- **Persistence** - Persistence is quite low for all of the series considered; on average, it is lower for prices (around 0.2) than for volumes (around 0.35).

- **Predictability** - The R^2 from an autoregressive model of order 1 can be interpreted as the (in sample) percentage of the series variance that can be predicted. Trade series show a very low predictable component; the R^2, on average, is 0.06 and 0.05 for export and import prices respectively, while it is slightly higher, 0.14 and 0.15, for export and import volumes. This makes the trade data hard to forecast, at least by using the traditional univariate time series model. One possibility to improve the forecastability is then to use information embedded in the cross-sectional dimension. The idea put forward in the paper is to augment the panel of trade variables with a block of macro variables, which have some degree of forecastability and, at the same time, are cross-correlated with the trade block. This is explained in the methodology section.

2.1   Trade Data Aggregation

This paper proposes a model that can deliver accurate forecasts of volumes and prices of euro area imports and exports. For the sake of simplicity bilateral trade variables are grouped in the following geographical areas: Brazil, Russia, India, and China (**BRIC**); Japan and South Korea (**Far East**); Switzerland, Denmark, Sweden, the U.K. and Turkey (**Europe**); the U.S. and Canada (**North America**); the countries that are members of the OPEC are grouped in the **Rest of the World**. Our dataset includes aggregated intra and aggregated extra euro area trade variables (import/export prices and volume). Such aggregated variables can be forecast directly or, alternatively, predicted by aggregating forecasts of the single geographical areas (the bottom-up approach). We show that the forecast accuracy of the bottom-up approach is superior or very close to the accuracy obtained by forecasting the aggregate series directly. This result is crucial, because it allows us to disentangle and

Table 1: Descriptive Statistics of the trade data

	EXPORT PRICES				IMPORT PRICES				EXPORT VOLUMES				IMPORT VOLUMES			
	μ	σ	$|\rho|$	R^2	μ	σ	$|\rho|$	R^2	μ	σ	$|\rho|$	R^2	μ	σ	$|\rho|$	R^2
Brazil	0.03	1.19	0.20	0.04	0.33	2.25	0.22	0.05	0.70	8.56	0.28	0.08	0.14	5.71	0.19	0.04
Russia	0.17	1.11	0.25	0.06	0.64	5.33	0.37	0.14	0.96	6.55	0.35	0.12	0.20	7.21	0.50	0.25
India	0.10	1.45	0.34	0.12	0.13	1.75	0.16	0.03	0.59	7.76	0.31	0.10	0.67	5.55	0.37	0.14
China	0.28	2.23	0.27	0.07	0.08	2.47	0.04	0.00	0.82	7.87	0.40	0.16	1.01	5.17	0.35	0.12
Japan	0.11	1.98	0.16	0.03	0.10	1.39	0.05	0.00	0.17	5.85	0.50	0.25	-0.05	4.40	0.33	0.11
Korea	0.12	2.36	0.34	0.12	-0.04	1.98	0.02	0.00	0.56	7.86	0.41	0.17	0.28	12.72	0.52	0.27
Switzerland	0.19	1.18	0.22	0.05	0.25	1.99	0.34	0.11	0.22	4.40	0.48	0.23	0.17	5.31	0.51	0.26
Denmark	0.15	1.13	0.39	0.15	0.18	1.58	0.31	0.09	0.16	3.34	0.32	0.10	0.07	6.28	0.55	0.29
Sweden	0.14	1.40	0.29	0.08	0.15	1.21	0.21	0.05	0.28	4.68	0.40	0.16	0.20	3.90	0.39	0.15
UK	0.17	1.17	0.06	0.00	0.30	1.55	0.04	0.00	0.19	3.49	0.43	0.18	-0.07	3.30	0.44	0.19
Turkey	0.16	1.17	0.30	0.09	0.16	1.07	0.06	0.00	0.60	6.68	0.05	0.00	0.39	2.76	0.08	0.01
US	0.22	2.01	0.27	0.08	0.25	2.08	0.07	0.00	0.30	5.00	0.43	0.18	0.08	3.20	0.27	0.07
Canada	0.12	2.01	0.34	0.11	0.19	2.58	0.13	0.02	0.31	5.94	0.43	0.18	-0.04	12.86	0.45	0.20
OPEC	0.16	1.05	0.21	0.05	0.62	5.15	0.43	0.18	0.69	6.77	0.54	0.29	-0.08	7.41	0.38	0.14
Extra	0.18	0.76	0.11	0.01	0.29	1.40	0.32	0.10	0.36	2.35	0.26	0.07	0.25	2.20	0.39	0.15
Intra	0.18	0.64	0.24	0.06	0.21	0.66	0.19	0.04	0.19	1.89	0.20	0.04	0.17	2.29	0.28	0.08
Rest of the World	0.28	2.94	0.02	0.00	0.46	3.74	0.15	0.02	0.23	5.46	0.38	0.15	0.10	5.50	0.30	0.09

Note: μ is the average, σ the standard deviation, $|\rho|$ (absolute value of) the autocorrelation coefficient of order one, the R^2 statistic is computed with an autoregressive model of order one with the constant.

measure the forecast contribution from geographical areas to the aggregate forecast (extra euro area) without paying a price in terms of aggregate forecasting performance.

The aggregations are constructed using time-varying weights: weights for volumes are computed by re-basing volume indices to the correspondent values as in 2000; weights for prices are computed using values in euro. Re-basing the volume indices to values as in 2000 also allows us to construct volumes for the Rest of the World and their respective prices (recall that we measure prices by the implicit deflators obtained by dividing the values in euro by volume indices).

Before moving to the forecasting exercise, we analyze the evolution of import and export shares over time; in addition, we show that the weighted average of the geographical growth rates accurately match the growth rate of the aggregate series. The top panel in Figure 2 shows the evolution of export shares for the five geographical areas. Different patterns can be observed over time: the export share to BRIC (∗ symbol) increases constantly from 5% in 2000 to 15% at the end of the period. The export share to North America declines from values close to 20% in 2000 to around 14% in the beginning of 2013 (◦ symbol). The same pattern can be observed for the export share to Europe: it declines from 35% in 2000 to just above 25% in 2013 (◇ symbol). The share of exports to the Rest of the World increases from 35% in 2000 to around 42% at the end of the sample period (× symbol). Finally, the export share of the Far East is relatively constant, just below 5% (+ symbol).

The bottom panel in Figure 2 shows the three-month-on-three-month (3Mo3M) extra euro area exports growth rate (red straight line) and its breakdown by geographical areas (colored bars). Given the low persistence and high volatility of the data, we prefer including graphs and forecasts in 3Mo3M growth rates. This aggregation facilitates the interpretation of the results, because it removes the high-frequency noise component of the data. The forecasting model is estimated on month-on-month transformations.

First and most importantly, the aggregation by geographical growth rates reconstructs the aggregate extra euro area export series (blue line) quite well, which is important because we can retrospectively analyze the contribution of the single countries/areas to the aggregate growth rate. For example, in the Great Recession period, all the areas substantially contributed to the drop in trade, while in the last years of our sample the contribution of Europe is negligible.

The top panel of Figure 3 shows the evolution for the euro area import shares from extra euro area countries. Euro area imports from BRIC (∗ symbol) grew from around 12% in 2000 to 25% in 2013, the share has remained constant since 2010. The euro area import share from North America declined from 15% in 2000 to around 10% in 2013 (o symbol). The euro area import share from our Europe block dropped from around 28% in 2000 to 21% at the end of the sample period (◊ symbol). The euro area import share from the Rest of the World has remained fairly constant over time, around 36% (× symbol). The euro area import share from our Far East block (+ symbol) has declined over time.

The bottom panel of Figure 3 shows the 3Mo3M extra euro area import growth rate (blue straight line) and a geographical breakdown. The aggregation by countries/areas closely matches the aggregate extra euro area series, also in this case. During the Great Recession, imports from different areas declined. Since 2011, the import pattern has been less synchronized: positive growth contributions from some areas have been counterbalanced by negative contributions from other areas.

Figures 4 and 5 analyze these trade patterns for total euro area exports and imports, dividing them in extra euro area and intra euro area. The share of extra euro area exports over total exports has increased over time from 48% in 2000 to around 57% in 2013 (Figure 4). A less steep, but similar trend is observed for extra euro area imports in Figure 5. In 2005, for both imports and exports, the intra and the extra euro area shares were equally split, at 50% each.

3   Econometric framework

As shown in Section 2, trade data are characterized by low persistence. In order to produce accurate forecasts of trade data, we exploit the cross correlation among trade variables and in turn their correlation with other macroeconomic data, which are published more timely than trade variables, i.e., they have a shorter publication delays. In order to exploit the cross correlation between macroeconomic and trade variables, we use a dynamic factor model. Factor models can summarize the co-movement of a potentially large set of observable data with few common factors. As shown in Giannone, Reichlin, and Small (2008), factor models work well for forecasting a variable (GDP in their case) that is characterized by substantial publication lag but, at the same time, displays a strong correlation with other data characterized by shorter publication delay (surveys, industrial production, etc). Given that trade variables are correlated with other macro variables but are published later than other macroeconomic variables, factor models are a natural tool to forecast them. The model is

$$y_t = \Lambda f_t + \xi_t \tag{1}$$

$$f_t = A_1 f_{t-1} + \cdots + A_p f_{t-p} + u_t \qquad u_t \sim N(0, Q) \tag{2}$$

$$\xi_t = B\xi_{t-1} + \epsilon_t \qquad \epsilon_t \sim N(0, R) \tag{3}$$

where $y_t = [y_{1,t}, y_{2,t}, \ldots, y_{n,t}]'$, $t = 1, \ldots, T$ denote a stationary n-dimensional vector process with zero mean and unit variance. This vector includes the observable data, i.e., trade and other macroeconomic variables; y_t depends on f_t, an r-dimensional vector of few unobserved common factors($r << n$) and n idiosyncratic components $\xi_t = [\xi_{1,t}, \xi_{2,t}, \ldots, \xi_{n,t}]'$, which are uncorrelated with f_t at all leads and lags. Λ is an $n \times r$ matrix of factor loadings. It is also assumed that the common factors f_t follow a stationary vector autoregressive process of order p, where $A_1, \ldots, A_p$ are $r \times r$ matrices of lagged coefficients. We model the dynamics of the idiosyncratic components ξ_t as a first-order autoregressive process, therefore, the matrix B is diagonal; ϵ_t is normally distributed and cross-sectionally uncorrelated (the variance-covariance matrix R is diagonal), i.e., y_t follows an exact factor model.

3.1   Estimation

As described above, our dataset as missing observations, not only at the end of the sample period (due to the different publication delays) but also at the beginning of the sample (due to the different time spans covered by the different series). In order to estimate the parameters of the model described by equations (1) to (3), given that we want to include restrictions on these parameters, and given the missing observations, we implement a Maximum Likelihood algorithm. More precisely, we make use of the algorithm proposed by Bańbura and Modugno (2014), i.e., a modification of the Expectation-Maximization (EM) algorithm that allows to estimate the parameters of the model described by equations (1) to (3) with arbitrary patterns of missing observations.

The EM algorithm is a natural choice for dealing with the issues that arise when estimating parameters of a dynamic factor model. The first issue is that f_t, the vector of common factors, is unobserved, which implies that the maximum likelihood estimates of the parameters are in general not available in closed form. Dempster, Laird, and Rubin (1977) introduced the EM algorithm as a general solution to problems for which latent states yield a likelihood function that is intractable. They propose express the likelihood in terms of both observed and unobserved state variables and iterating between two operations: (i) computing the expectation of the log-likelihood (sufficient statistics) conditional on the data using the parameter estimates from the previous iteration, and (ii) reestimating the parameters through the maximization of the expected log-likelihood. In the case of our model this algorithm simplifies to an iteration between the two steps until convergence is achieved, while correcting at each step for the uncertainty associated with the estimation of the common factors (Watson and Engle, 1983; Shumway and Stoffer, 1982).

The second issue is due to the large number of series included in the panel. When n is large, the assumption of an exact factor structure, i.e., the matrix R is diagonal, can be the source of misspecification, given that some local cross correlation can still survive after controlling for the common factors. However, Doz, Giannone, and Reichlin (2007) show that the effects of this misspecification on the estimation of the common factors is negligible when the sample size (T) and the cross-section (n) are large. They show that the factors extracted under the assumption of zero cross correlation among the idiosyncratic components span the same space of factors extracted assuming that the cross correlation among the idiosyncratic components is weak. Moreover, they show that the estimator is feasible when n is large and easily implementable using the Kalman smoother and the EM algorithm as in traditional factor analysis.

3.2 Restrictions on the parameters

One of the advantages of the maximum likelihood approach, with respect to nonparametric methods based on principal components, is that it allows us to impose restrictions on the parameters in a relatively straightforward manner.

Bork (2009) and Bork, Dewachter, and Houssa (2009) show how to modify the maximization step of EM algorithm described Watson and Engle (1983) in order to impose restrictions of the form $H_\Lambda \text{vec}(\Lambda) = \kappa_\Lambda$ for the model described in equations (1) to (3). Bańbura and Modugno (2014) show how those restrictions can be imposed in the presence of an arbitrary pattern of missing data.

We impose restrictions on the factor loadings matrix (Λ) in order to identify the factors in our model. The factor loadings are restricted to be equal to zero if the corresponding data series are not included in the group that identifies a factor. We assume there are four factors related to import prices, export prices, import volume, and export volume dynamics:

1. f^1 is the factor capturing the co-movement among export volumes, EA trade partners PMIs and industrial productions, and the real effective exchange rate.

2. f^2 is the factor capturing the co-movement among the real effective exchange rate, all import volumes, and the real euro area macroeconomic variables, i.e., industrial production, retail sales, and the unemployment rate.

3. f^3 is the factor capturing the co-movement among the real effective exchange rate, all export prices and the nominal euro area macroeconomic variables, i.e., CPI and PPI.

4. f^4 is the factor capturing the co-movement among the real effective exchange rate, all import prices and the euro area trade partners PPIs.

The exchange rate is the only variable that is included in the four factors. In Table 3 of the appendix, we report the block structure.

In order to understand if the information content of macroeconomic variables increases the forecasting accuracy for trade variables, we compare the model described so far with a similar model that includes only trade variables. This second model is also characterized by four factors, defined as follows:

1. f_{ot}^1 is the factor capturing the co-movement among all export volumes.

2. f_{ot}^2 is the factor capturing the co-movement among all import volumes.

3. f_{ot}^3 is the factor capturing the co-movement among all export prices.

4. f_{ot}^4 is the factor capturing the co-movement among all import prices.

The block structure for the trade variables is described in the appendix (Table 4). Note that we do not impose any restriction to the transition equation (2): the factors interact with each other through the vector autoregressive process.

3.3 Forecasting

Forecasts are generated from the parameter estimates of the model described in equations (1) to (3) $\hat{\theta} = [\hat{\Lambda}, \hat{A}_1, ..., \hat{A}_p, \hat{B}, \hat{R}, \hat{Q}]$ and the dataset Ω_v. The forecasts are defined as conditional expectations of the target variable $y_{i,t}$, obtained at time v, given the information set Ω_v. Notice that v refers to the point in time at which we produce the forecast and v can refer to any time frequency; we will assume that v is monthly, i.e. the forecast performance

11

is evaluated every month. If $t < v$ we are backcasting, if $t = v$ we are nowcasting and if $t > v$ we are forecasting. Forecasts are computed as:

$$\mathbb{E}_{\hat{\theta}}\left[y_{i,t}|\Omega_v\right] = \hat{\Lambda}_{i.}\mathbb{E}_{\hat{\theta}}\left[f_t|\Omega_v\right] + \mathbb{E}_{\hat{\theta}}\left[\xi_{i,t}|\Omega_v\right], \qquad\qquad y_{i,t} \notin \Omega_v, \qquad\qquad (4)$$

where $\hat{\Lambda}_{i.}$ denotes the ith row of $\hat{\Lambda}$, the maximum likelihood estimate of Λ. $\mathbb{E}_{\hat{\theta}}\left[f_t|\Omega_v\right]$ and $\mathbb{E}_{\hat{\theta}}\left[\xi_{i,t}|\Omega_v\right]$ are obtained by applying the Kalman filter (for forecasting) and smoother (for nowcasting and backcasting) to the state-space representation, equations (1) to (3). Finally, $\mathbb{E}_{\hat{\theta}}\left[\xi_{i,t}|\Omega_v\right] \neq 0$, given that, in our case, the idiosyncratic components follow a first-order autoregressive process.

4 Forecast evaluation

We evaluate the forecast performance of our model via a pseudo-real-time out-of-sample simulation on the sample January 2006 to April 2013: the forecast horizon varies from -2 to 0, where -2 and -1 are the previous two months' and one month's backcasts respectively, and 0 the current month's nowcast. We produce these estimates every month, with a dataset characterized by a "ragged edge" structure that mimics the information available at the end of each month. The vintage of data on which our estimates are based was downloaded on July 31 2013. For example, let us assume that we start the forecast evaluation on January 31 2006. On this day, trade data relative to Denmark, Sweden and Great Britain are available until October 2005, while all the other trade data are available up to November 2005. Macroeconomic variables are more timely: PMIs and IPs of Russia and the United States are available for December 2005, while the IPs for all the other non-euro area countries are available up to November 2005. PPIs are all available up to December 2005, except for Brazil, for which data is available up to November 2005. Euro area macroeconomic data are all available up to November 2005, but the exchange rate is available up to December 2005. This structure is exactly replicated at each forecast iteration to implement a pseudo-real-time exercise.

Forecasts are evaluated by the mean squared forecast error (MSFE) statistic defined as

$$MSFE_{t_0}^{t_1} = \frac{1}{t_1 - t_0 + 1}\sum_{t=t_0}^{t_1}\left(\hat{Y}_{t+h|t} - Y_{t+h}\right)^2, \qquad\qquad (5)$$

12

where $\hat{Y}_{t+h|t}$ is the backcast or nowcast ($h = -2, h = -1$ and $h = 0$) of the target variables and Y_{t+h} are the ex-post realized values; t_0 and t_1 are the starting and ending forecast evaluation periods.

The forecasting exercise has two aims: first, to understand the marginal forecasting power of the macro variables and, second, to compare the relative performance of the aggregate vs. disaggregate forecast.

Results are reported as the ratio of the MSFE generated by the proposed models to the MSFE obtained with a benchmark naïve model, which is the constant growth model. A ratio smaller than 1 indicates that the factor model improved on the benchmark.

Table 2 compares the results for the two factor models without macro variables (panel A) and with macro variables (panel B). All the forecasts are computed by the bottom-up approach, that is, by aggregating forecasts from the different geographical areas. The factor model with only trade variables displays a much better two-month backcast performance ($h = -2$) compared with the the naïve model (the relative MSFE is smaller than one). The performance is in line with that of the benchmark for the one-month backcast ($h = -1$), is slightly worse for export and import prices (1.02 and 1.08, respectively), and is slightly better for import and export volume (0.99 and 0.93, respectively). The performance deteriorates for the import and export prices nowcast ($h = 0$), and is identical to that of the benchmark model for export volumes; it improves for import volumes by 10% with respect to the naïve model.

When we include macro variables in our model, there is a generalized improvement of the forecasting performance with respect to both the naïve benchmark and the model with only trade variables. Relative MSFEs in panel B are always smaller than those in panel A, the only exceptions being export and import volumes for $h = 0$, which are slightly higher.

Panel C in table 2 compares the relative performance of disaggregated forecasts with the aggregated forecasts. The latter is generated by computing the predictions of extra euro area trade directly using the aggregate series. The results show that the performance of the bottom-up approach is similar to that of the direct forecast. On average, the relative MSFE statistics are around 1. This result is important, because it allows us to decompose the forecast contributions to the aggregate series by geographical areas.

Figure 6 to Figure 9 show the forecast results. Panel 1 to 3 in Figure 6 shows the backcast performance (panels 1 and 2 for $h = -2$ and $h = -1$ respectively) and the nowcast performance (panel 3) for 3Mo3M exports prices. The colored bars refer to the contribution of a geographical area to the aggregate extra euro area export prices series (blue dashed

Table 2: Relative MSFE: Extra Euro Area Trade

| | Trade Variables Only: PANEL A | | | |
	Export Prices	Import Prices	Export Volumes	Import Volumes
h=-2	0.28	0.36	0.43	0.47
h=-1	1.02	1.08	0.99	0.93
h=0	1.06	1.21	1.00	0.90
	Trade and Macro Variables: PANEL B			
	Export Prices	Import Prices	Export Volumes	Import Volumes
h=-2	0.22	0.17	0.37	0.42
h=-1	0.86	0.79	0.86	0.89
h=0	0.80	0.87	1.13	0.95
	Disaggregate vs Aggregate Forecasts: PANEL C			
	Export Prices	Import Prices	Export Volumes	Import Volumes
h=-2	0.83	1.04	0.88	1.07
h=-1	1.00	1.17	0.93	0.89
h=0	1.02	1.05	0.99	0.97

Note: PANEL A reports the relative Mean Square Forecast Error (MSFE) between the MSFE obtained with an baseline constant growth model (denominator) and that obtained with the factor model computed on a panel with only trade variables (numerator). In PANEL B the factor model includes trade and macro variables; the numbers report the relative MSFE as in PANEL A. PANEL C shows the ratio of the MSFE obtained aggregating the forecast for each single area to the MSFE obtained forecasting directly the aggregated series. A ratio below 1 indicates that the model at the numerator has a more accurate forecasting performance. $h = -2$, $h = -1$ and $h = 0$ denote the forecast horizons; in this case they refer to two months ago backcast, one month ago backcast and nowcast respectively. The forecasting period is January 2007 to April 2013.

line). The red line shows the 3Mo3M realized value. The export prices forecasts are quite accurate, and track the realized series relatively well; the performance tends to deteriorate over the forecast horizon, from $h = -2$ to $h = 0$. The relative forecast contributions show that the forecast deflation in imports prices, over the last part of the sample, is mainly due to the North America forecast.

Figure 7 is similar to Figure 6: it shows the forecast patterns for extra euro area export volumes. In this case, the forecasts are rather accurate, that is the forecasts capture the great trade collapse in the middle of the sample, and, as expected, the accuracy deteriorates with the forecast horizon. In terms of forecast contribution, the Rest of the World and Europe are the main components of the aggregate series; forecast contributions from different geographical areas tend to co-move closely. However, this pattern is broken over the last part of the sample, where contributions from different areas to the aggregate forecast seem to be more erratic.

Figure 8 shows the results for import prices. Forecasts track the realized series well. Contributions to the aggregate forecasts tend to co-move. The most important components for the aggregate dynamics are import prices developments from BRIC and the Rest of the World.

Finally, Figures 9 displays the results for import volumes. The overall performance looks quite good. The main contributors to the overall figure are, as in the previous figure, BRIC and the Rest of the World. Imports from Europe played a nontrivial role in forecasting the Great Trade Collapse.

5   Conditional forecast

The econometric model specified in this paper can also be used to produce conditional forecasts that is, to evaluate the dynamics of a target variable conditional on the future path of some other variables. The state space formulation of the factor model provides a natural framework to address this kind of exercise (see Bańbura, Giannone, and Lenza, 2014). We consider conditional forecast for two reasons: first we want to examine how reliable our model is for producing trade data paths conditional on macroeconomic variables. Second, we want to quantify the contribution of the most important euro area trading partners (regions) to aggregate extra euro area developments.

In order to asses the reliability of our model to generate paths of trade variables conditional on macro variables, we conduct a natural experiment. Namely, we estimate the parameters of the model with data available until December 2007 and then "feed" the Kalman filter with those parameters and with the observed macro variables from January 2008 to April 2013 to generate the conditional path of trade variables.

This exercise is informative: by comparing the conditional forecasts of the trade variables with their realized values, we provide an indirect measure of the importance of macro variables in driving trade dynamics. In addition, the exercise also provides an indication of the ability of the model to assess the effect of macroeconomic scenarios on the trade variables.

Figure 10 and Figure 11 show the results for export and import volumes, respectively, and for the four different geographical areas (BRIC, Far East, Europe and North America). Results for the Rest of the World block are reported in Figure 12.[5] In all the charts, the red line refers to the 3Mo3M conditional growth rate dynamics, the blue line is the 3Mo3M ex-post realized values and the green line is the 3Mo3M unconditional path. The first panel of Figure 10 shows the conditional path of (3Mo3M) exports volumes to BRIC (red line).

---

[5]We keep the trade weights constant at December 2007 values to aggregate the series from January 2008 to April 2013.

In general, the simulated series (red line) track the actual path (blue line) well; they do not fully capture the depth of the drop in exports during 2009, but none the less shows a substantial decline. Export dynamics to the Far East (top-right panel) are also well captured by the conditional series (red line); both the drop in 2009 and the general contour are well fitted. The two bottom panels show the conditional paths of exports to our Europe block and North America; the two series describe trade dynamics well, even if the trade collapse in 2009 is not fully captured.

Figure 11 shows the conditional paths of import volumes. The simulation exercise shows that the import drop in 2009 is well fitted in the four geographical areas; the general pattern is also well tracked, although there is a slight upward bias for the BRIC series (top-left panel) and the Far East series (top-right panel).

Figure 12 shows the results for the Rest of the World. The top panel displays the results for exports. The conditional series (red line) exhibits a poor fit; it does not co-move much with the observed values (blue line). This result can be explained by the lack of macroeconomic series in our dataset for this "residual" region: macroeconomic data are a good proxy of the external demand component, which is correlated to exports.

The bottom panel in Figure 12 shows the simulation for imports (red line). In this case, the conditional forecast desplays a quite accurate fit. It captures the drop in 2009 and the general contour well.

The second simulation exercise addresses the effect of an increase of the external demand components on extra euro area exports. It is designed in the following way: first, we estimate the model until December 2007 and compute the unconditional forecast of the variables in the model. Second, we increase the unconditional forecast of the external demand components, proxied by IP and PMI series, by 5% . Third, we estimate the implied path of the extra euro area exports, after December 2007, conditional on the (5%) increased path of external demand components. Fourth, we compute the difference between conditional and unconditional paths, which is essentially a generalized impulse response function (IRF). Figure 13 reports results for a 5% increase of all of the components of external demand. In the same figure, we report the results obtained for a 5% increase of the external demand components relative to one of the four geographical area (Europe, North America, BRIC, and Far East), which allows us to evaluate the importance of different geographical areas for the extra euro area exports.

The blue straight line (all) shows that a permanent increase of 5% of the external demand would have generated, on impact, an increase of 0.22 percentage point on the baseline un-

16

conditional forecast. The generalized IRF peaks the third month with a deviation from the unconditional forecast of about 0.57 percentage point. It stabilizes at around 0.08 percentage point after about 10 months.

IRFs from specific areas have similar dynamics, although the impact on extra euro area exports is weaker. The IRFs all peak in the third month to stabilize after 10 periods. Over the sample analyzed, a 5% increase of demand from BRIC ($\diamond$ symbol) generates a permanent increase of about 0.05% of extra euro area exports in the long run; a 5% increase of demand from Europe (dashed line) generates an increase of about 0.027%, while an increase of the same magnitude from North America (. symbol) is estimated to raise extra euro area exports approximately by 0.019 percentage point. The long-run effect from the Far East ($\circ$ symbol) is negligible.

6   Conclusions

In this paper, we study and forecast trade dynamics in the euro area. We use the factor model proposed by Bańbura and Modugno (2014). This model is a flexible tool to extract information from datasets characterized by arbitrary patterns of missing data. Furthermore, it allows for restrictions on the parameter space, which is essential for the identification of the factors in the model.

We focus on backcasting and nowcasting extra euro area import volumes, import prices, export price, export volumes, and their geographical subcomponents. In a pseudo-out-of-sample evaluation exercise starting in January 2006, we show that the model with trade and macro variables improves on the forecastability of a model with only trade variables. The more timely information of macro variables delivers an improvement in forecast accuracy.

In addition, we show that aggregating forecasts from euro area trading regions (bottom-up approach) delivers predictions as accurate as those obtained by forecasting directly the extra euro are series ("direct" approach). This result is important, because it allows us to disentangle the contribution to the extra euro area trade forecast of different world regions.

Finally, we set up two counterfactual exercises. In the first, we show that macro variables track trade dynamics well; this result implies that future trade paths can be inferred by future macro paths, which are more predictable. In the second, we evaluate the effect of an increase of the external demand on extra euro area trade. Results point to a permanent shift of 0.08 percentage point after an increase of 5% in the external demand.

17

References

BAŃBURA, M., D. GIANNONE, AND M. LENZA (2014): "Conditional Forecasts and Scenario Analysis with Vector Autoregressions for Large Cross-Sections," *International Journal of Forecasting*, forthcoming.

BAŃBURA, M., D. GIANNONE, M. MODUGNO, AND L. REICHLIN (2013): "Now-casting and the real-time data flow," *Handbook of Economic Forecasting*, 2, 195–236.

BAŃBURA, M., D. GIANNONE, AND L. REICHLIN (2011): "Nowcasting," *Oxford Handbook on Economic Forecasting*.

BAŃBURA, M., AND M. MODUGNO (2014): "Maximum Likelihood Estimation of Factor Models on Datasets with Arbitrary Pattern of Missing Data," *Journal of Applied Econometrics*, 29(1), 133–160.

BORK, L. (2009): "Estimating US Monetary Policy Shocks Using a Factor-Augmented Vector Autoregression: An EM Algorithm Approach," CREATES Research Papers 2009-11, School of Economics and Management, University of Aarhus.

BORK, L., H. DEWACHTER, AND R. HOUSSA (2009): "Identification of Macroeconomic Factors in Large Panels," CREATES Research Papers 2009-43, School of Economics and Management, University of Aarhus.

BURGERT, M., AND S. DÉES (2009): "Forecasting World Trade: Direct Versus "Bottom-Up" Approaches," *Open Economies Review*, 20(3), 385–402.

DEMPSTER, A., N. LAIRD, AND D. RUBIN (1977): "Maximum Likelihood Estimation From Incomplete Data," *Journal of the Royal Statistical Society*, 14, 1–38.

DOZ, C., D. GIANNONE, AND L. REICHLIN (2007): "A two-step estimator for large approximate dynamic factor models based on Kalman filtering," CEPR Discussion Papers 6043, C.E.P.R. Discussion Papers.

GIANNONE, D., L. REICHLIN, AND D. SMALL (2008): "Nowcasting: The real-time informational content of macroeconomic data," *Journal of Monetary Economics*, 55(4), 665–676.

HERVÉ, K., N. PAIN, P. RICHARDSON, F. SÉDILLOT, AND P.-O. BEFFY (2011): "The OECD's new global model," *Economic Modelling*, 28(1-2), 589–601.

JAKAITIENE, A., AND S. DÉES (2012): "Forecasting the World Economy in the Short Term," *The World Economy*, 35(3), 331–350.

KECK, A., A. RAUBOLD, AND A. TRUPPIA (2009): "Forecasting international trade: A time series approach," *OECD Journal: Journal of Business Cycle Measurement and Analysis*, 2009(2), 157–176.

LIN, L., AND M. XIA (2009): "A Novel Fuzzy Evolutionary Algorithm for Forecasting of International Trade in Dynamical Environment," in *Services Science, Management and Engineering, 2009.*, pp. 325–328.

MARCELLINO, M., J. H. STOCK, AND M. W. WATSON (2003): "Macroeconomic forecasting in the Euro area: Country specific versus area-wide information," *European Economic Review*, 47(1), 1–18.

RIAD, N., L. ERRICO, C. HENN, C. SABOROWSKI, M. SAITO, AND J. TURUNEN (2012): "Changing Patterns of Global Trade," *IMF Policy Paper*, 12(1).

SHUMWAY, R., AND D. STOFFER (1982): "An approach to time series smoothing and forecasting using the EM algorithm," *Journal of Time Series Analysis*, 3, 253–264.

WATSON, M. W., AND R. F. ENGLE (1983): "Alternative algorithms for the estimation of dynamic factor, mimic and varying coefficient regression models," *Journal of Econometrics*, 23, 385–400.

YU, L., S. WANG, AND K. K. LAI (2008): "Forecasting China's Foreign Trade Volume with a Kernel-Based Hybrid Econometric-AI Ensemble Learning Approach," *Journal of Systems Science and Complexity*, 21(1), 1.

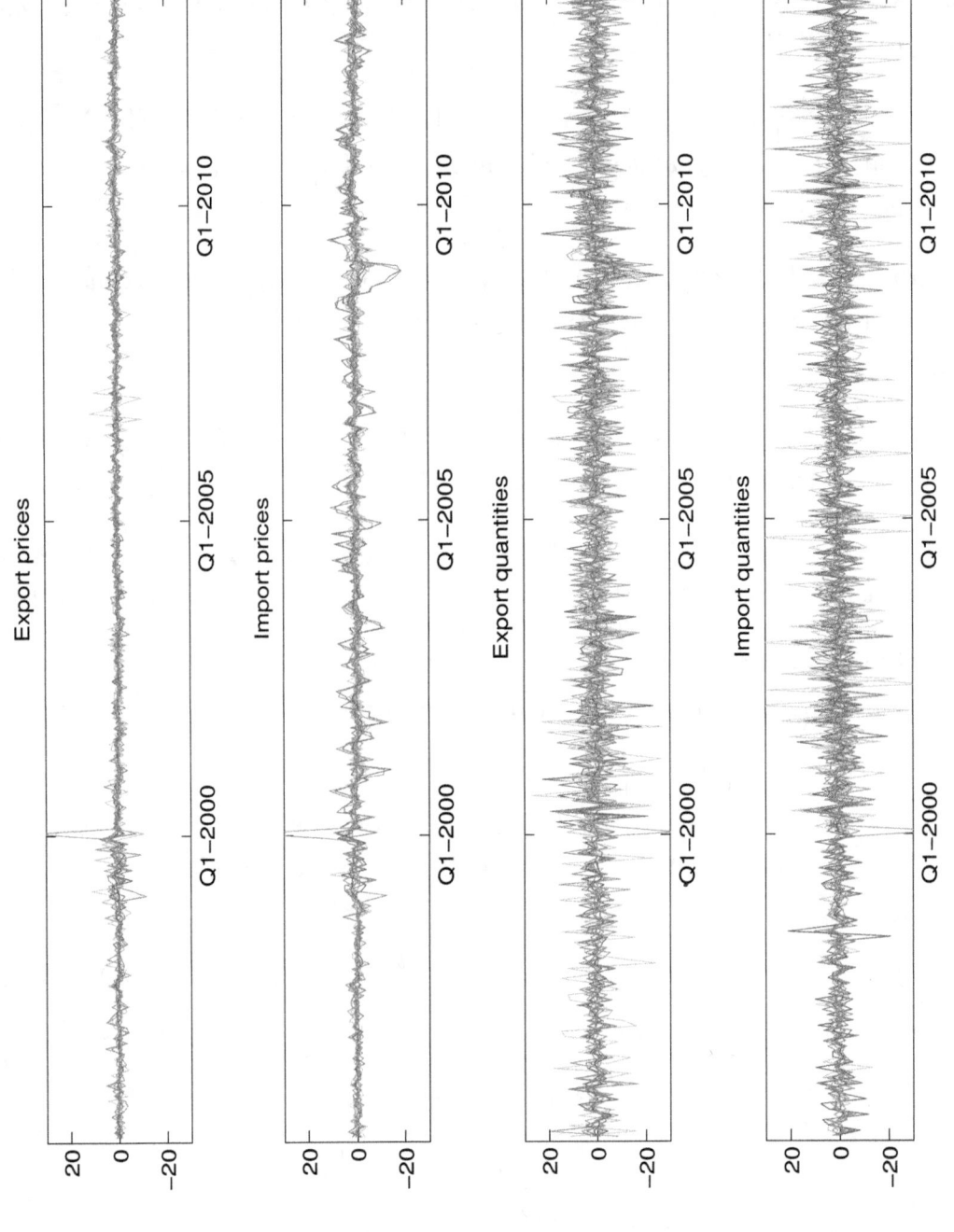

Figure 1: Trade variables

Note: Trade variables included in the analysis are month-on-month growth rates.

Figure 2: Contribution to extra euro area export volumes growth by geographical breakdown

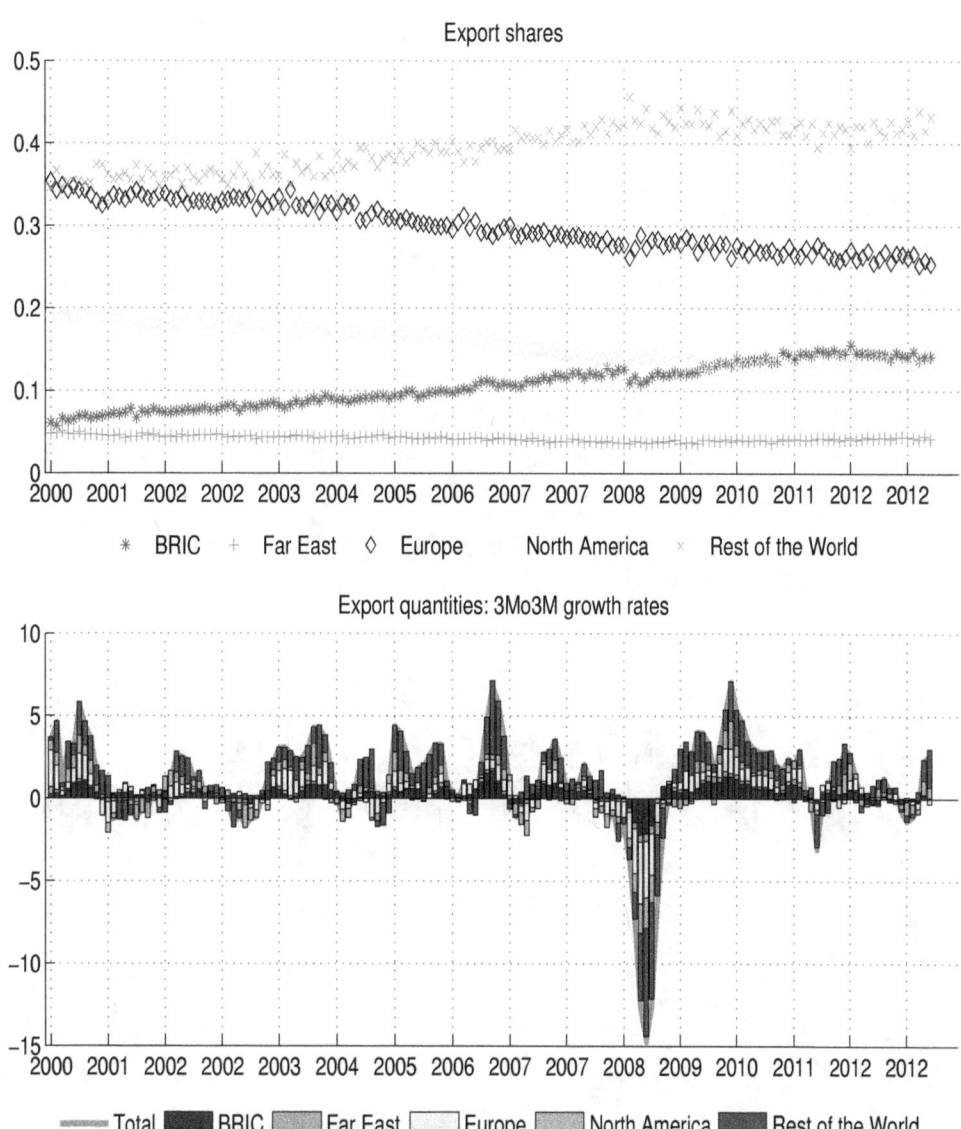

Note: Top panel - extra euro area export shares by geographical areas. Bottom panel - three-month-on-three-month (3Mo3M) extra euro area export volume growth rate (red straight line) and the relative growth rate contributions by geographical areas (colored bars).

Figure 3: Contribution to extra euro area import volumes growth by geographical breakdown

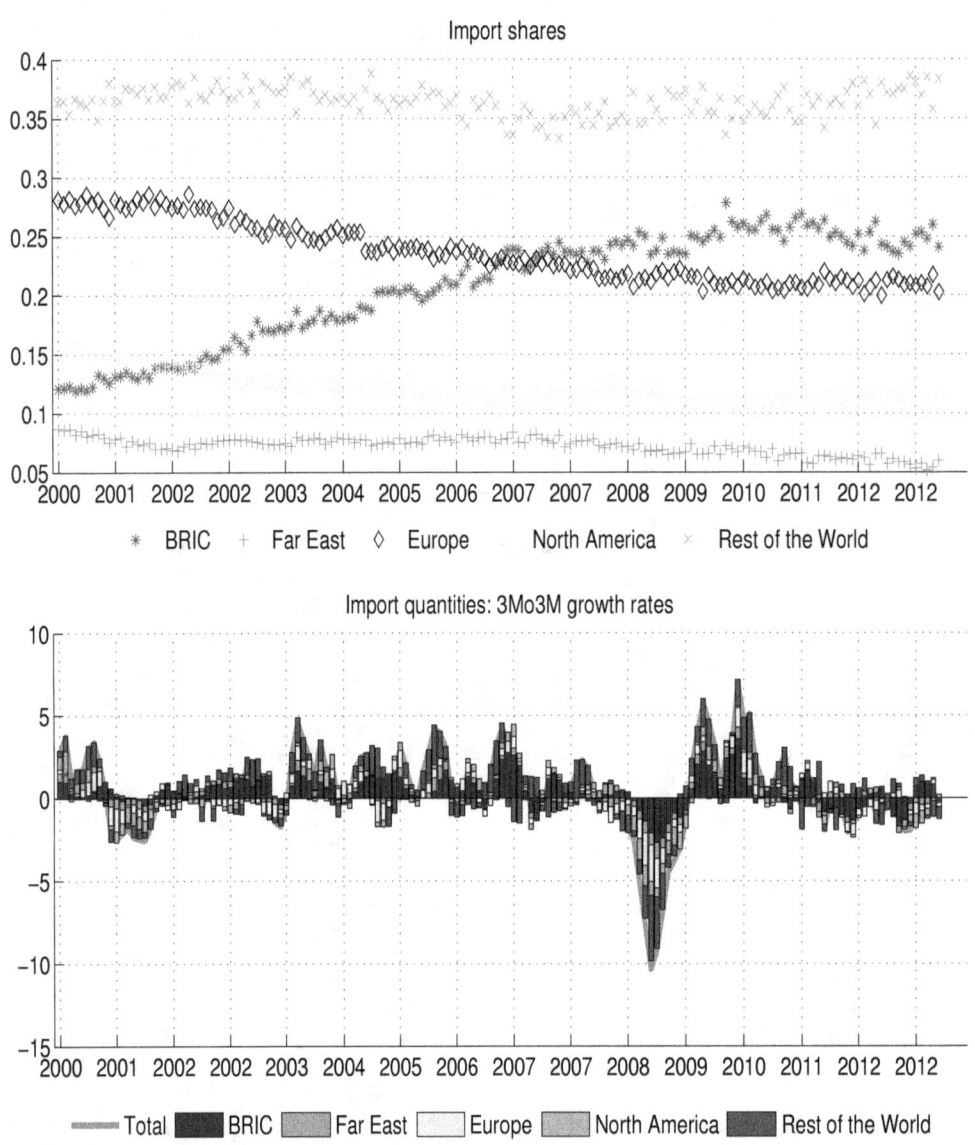

Note: Top panel - extra euro area import shares by geographical areas. Bottom panel - three-month-on-three-month (3Mo3M) extra euro area import volume growth rate (red straight line) and the relative growth rate contributions by geographical areas (colored bars).

Figure 4: Contribution to euro area export volumes growth: extra and intra decomposition

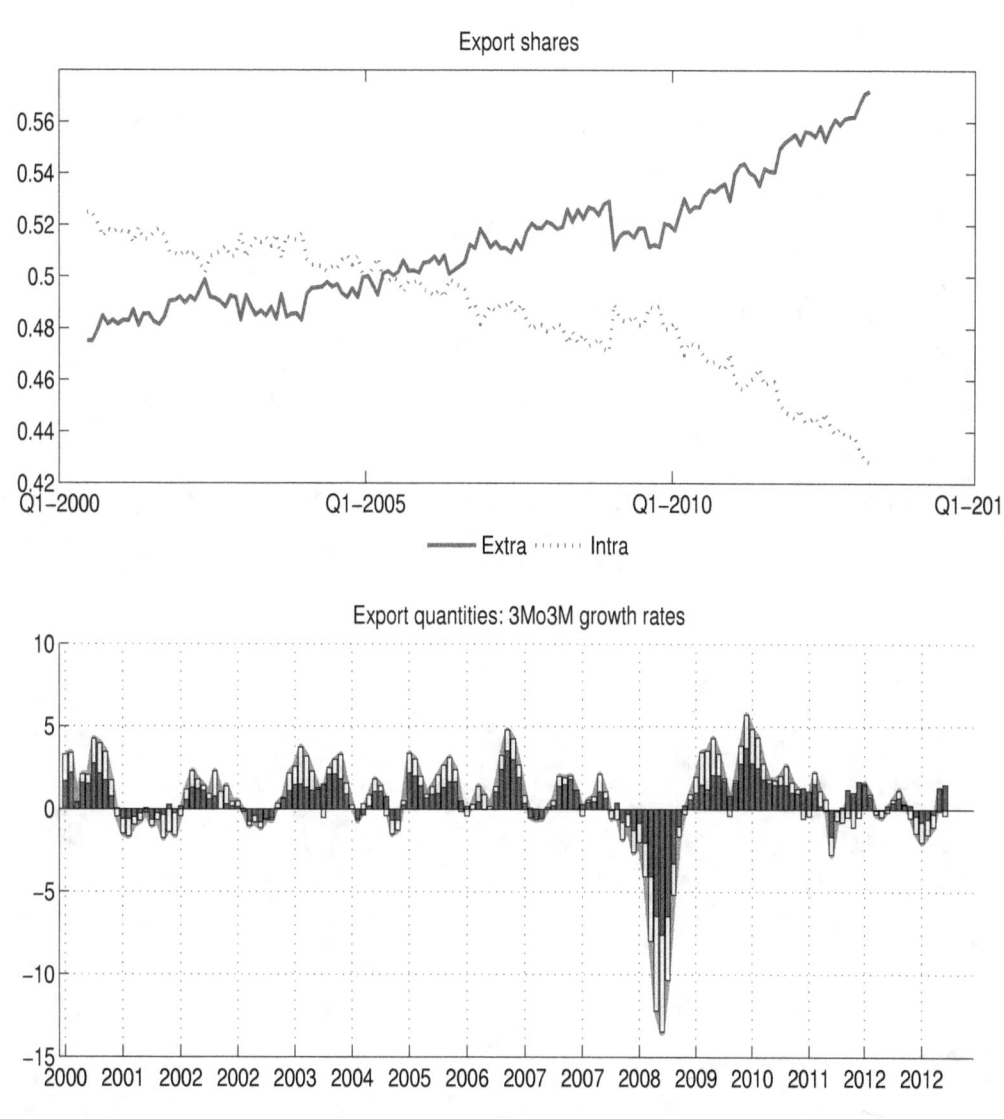

Note: Top panel - extra and intra euro area export shares. Bottom panel - three-month-on-three-month (3Mo3M) euro area export quantity growth rate (red straight line) and the extra and intra relative growth rate contributions (colored bars).

Figure 5: Contribution to euro area import volumes growth: extra and intra decomposition

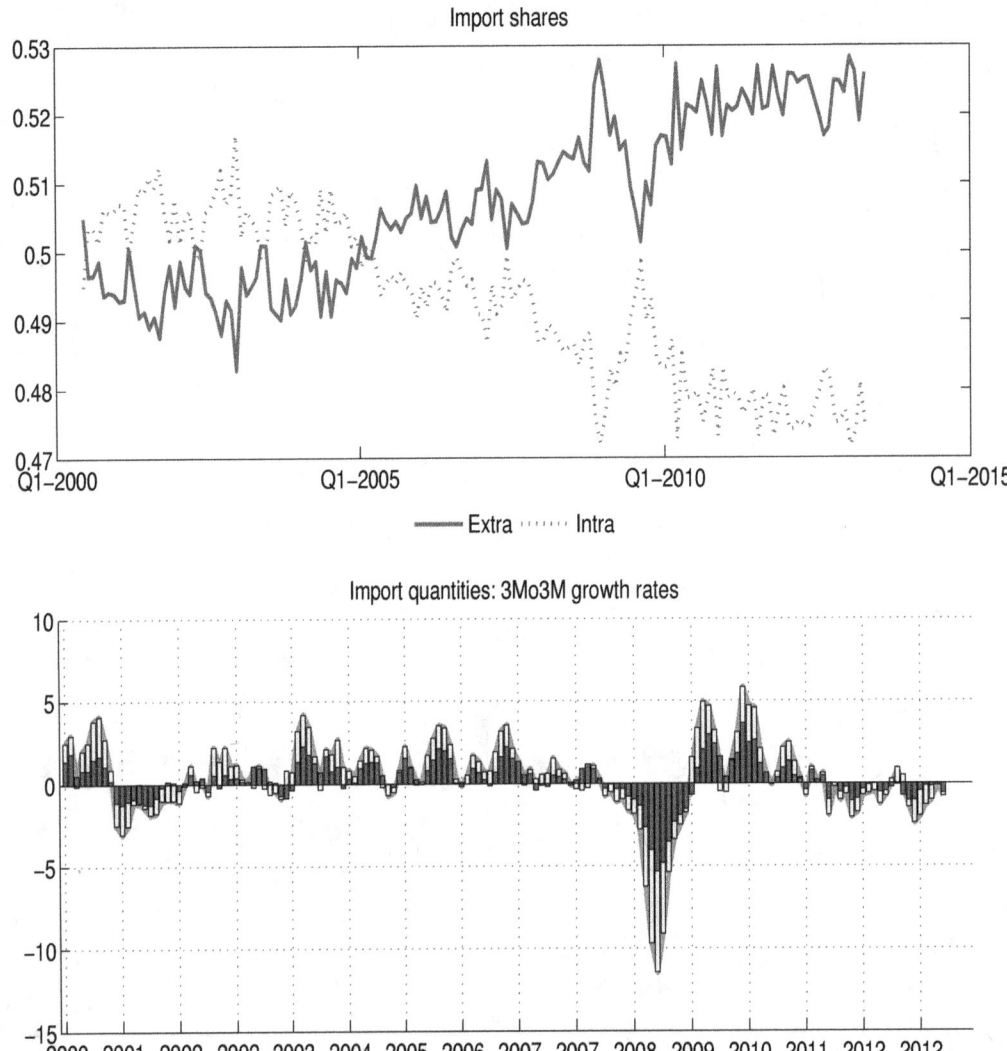

Note: Top panel - extra and intra euro area import shares. Bottom panel - three-month-on-three-month (3Mo3M) euro area import volume growth rate (red straight line) and the extra and intra relative growth rate contributions (colored bars).

Figure 6: Export prices

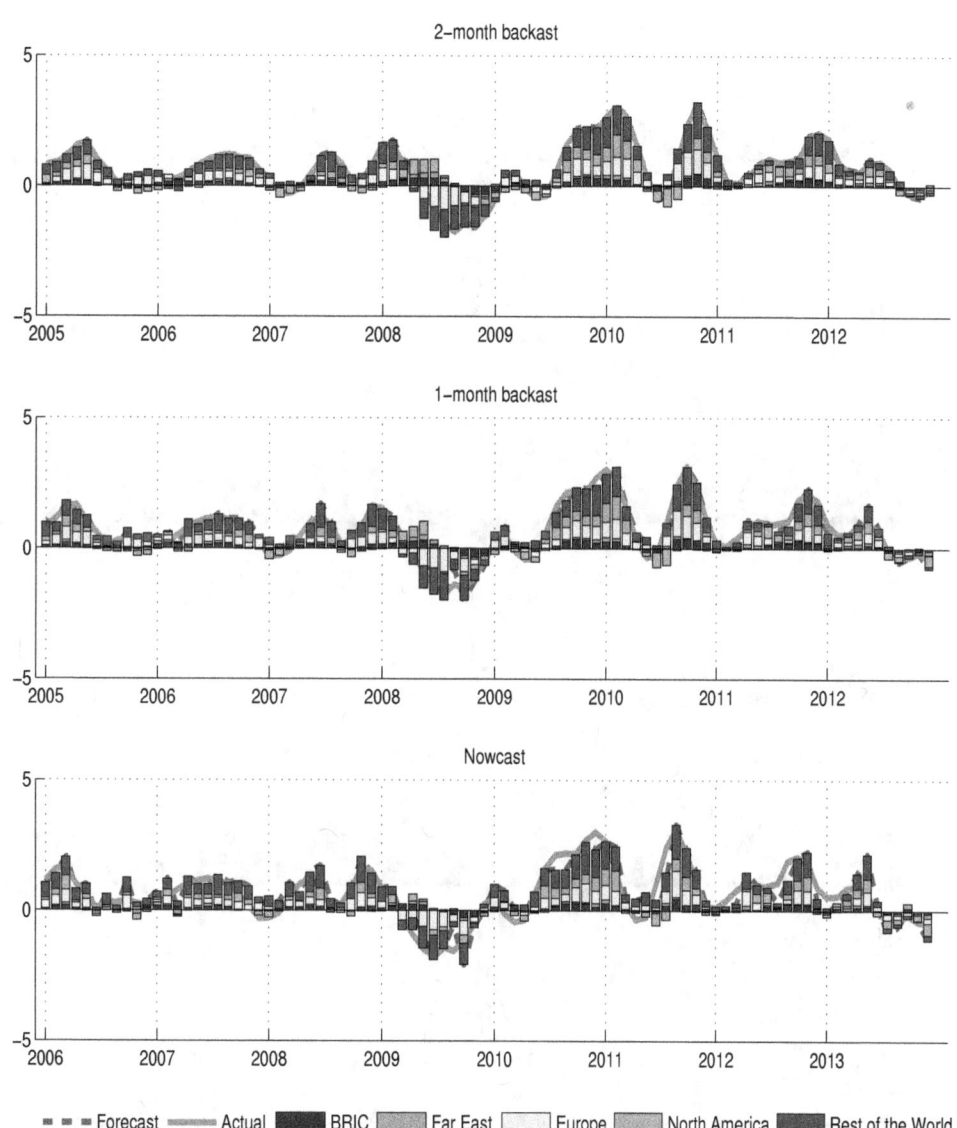

Note: three-month-on-three-month (3Mo3M) growth rates - extra euro export prices forecasts. The dashed blue line is the aggregated extra euro area forecast. The colored bars are the forecast contributions from different geographical areas. The red straight line is the ex-post realized value. First panel: two-month backcast - Second panel: one-month backcast - Third panel: nowcast.

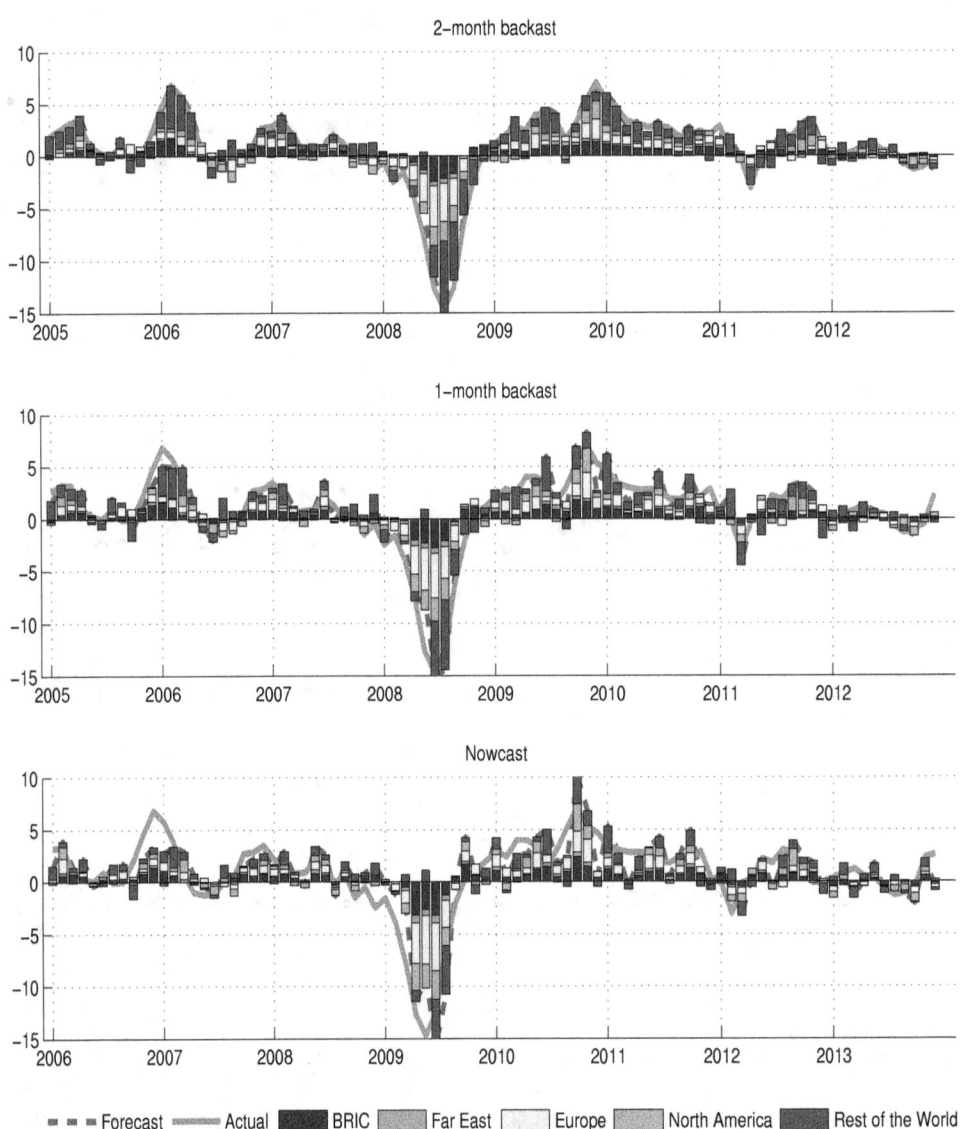

Figure 7: Export volumes

Note: three-month-on-three-month (3Mo3M) growth rates - extra euro export volumes forecasts. The dashed, blue line is the aggregated extra euro area forecast. The colored bars are the forecast contributions from different geographical areas. The red straight line is the ex-post realized value. First panel: two-month backcast - Second panel: one-month backcast - Third panel: nowcast.

Figure 8: Import prices

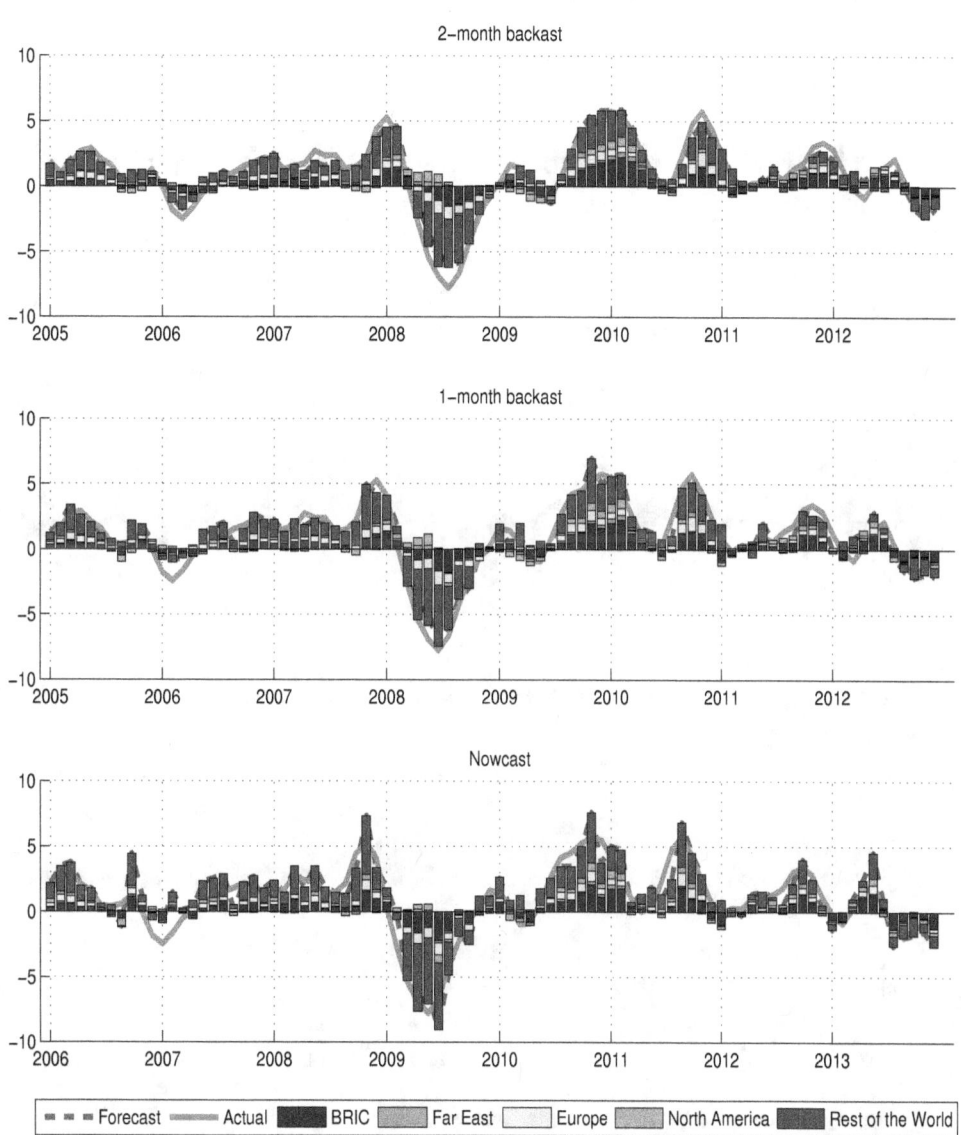

Note: three-month-on-three-month (3Mo3M) growth rates - extra euro import prices forecasts. The dashed blue line is the aggregated extra euro area forecast. The colored bars are the forecast contributions from different geographical areas. The red straight line is the ex-post realized value. First panel: two-month backcast - Second panel: one-month backcast - Third panel: nowcast.

Figure 9: Import volumes

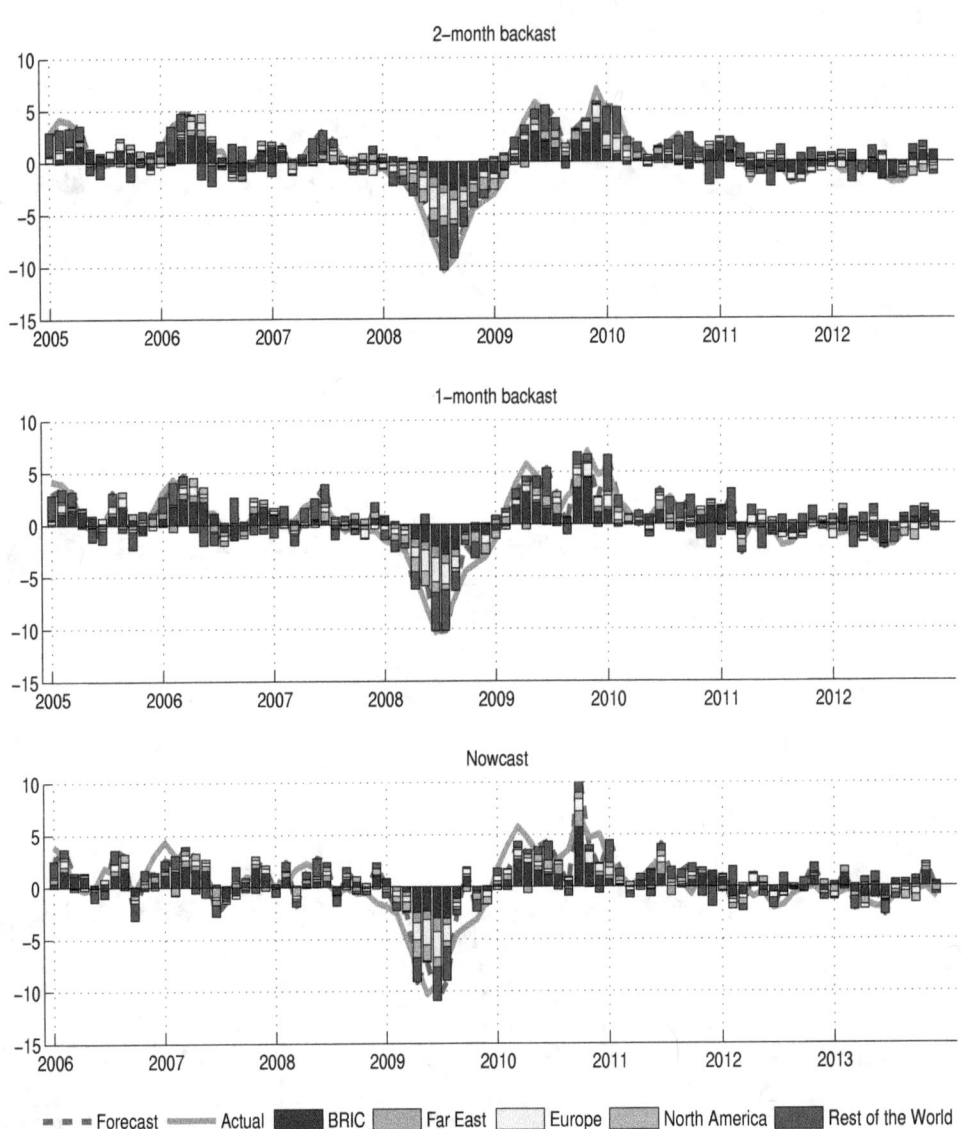

Note: three-month-on-three-month (3Mo3M) growth rates - extra euro import volumes forecasts. The dashed blue line is the aggregated extra euro area forecast. The colored bars are the forecast contributions from different geographical areas. The red straight line is the ex-post realized value. First panel: two-month backcast - Second panel: one-month backcast - Third panel: nowcast.

Figure 10: Conditional path for export volumes

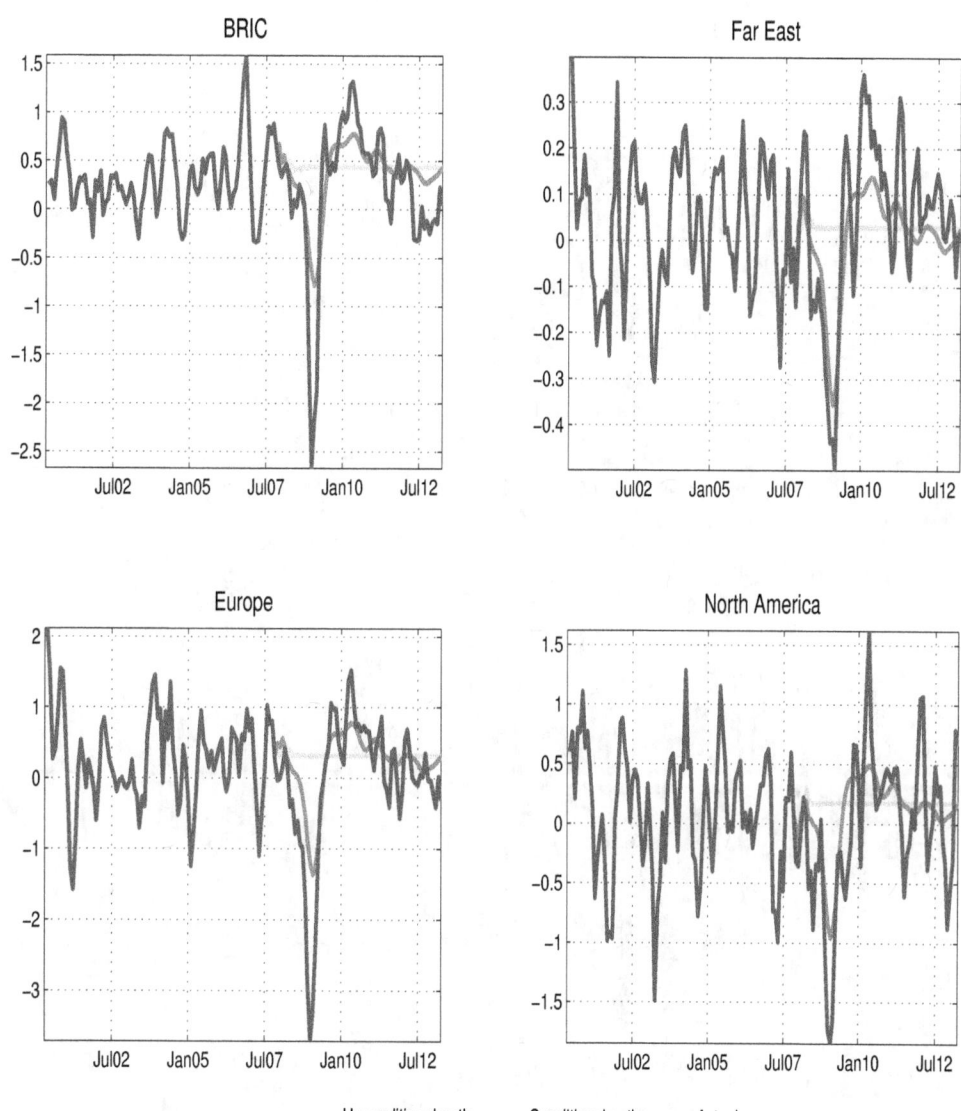

Note: Simulated extra euro area export volumes path over the sample November 2007 to April 2013; trade dynamics are conditional on the realized macro values from November 2007 to April 2013 and on the parameters estimated with the data available at the end of December 2007. The four subplots refer to different geographical areas. Values are in three-month-on-three-month (3Mo3M) growth rates.

29

Figure 11: Conditional path for import volumes

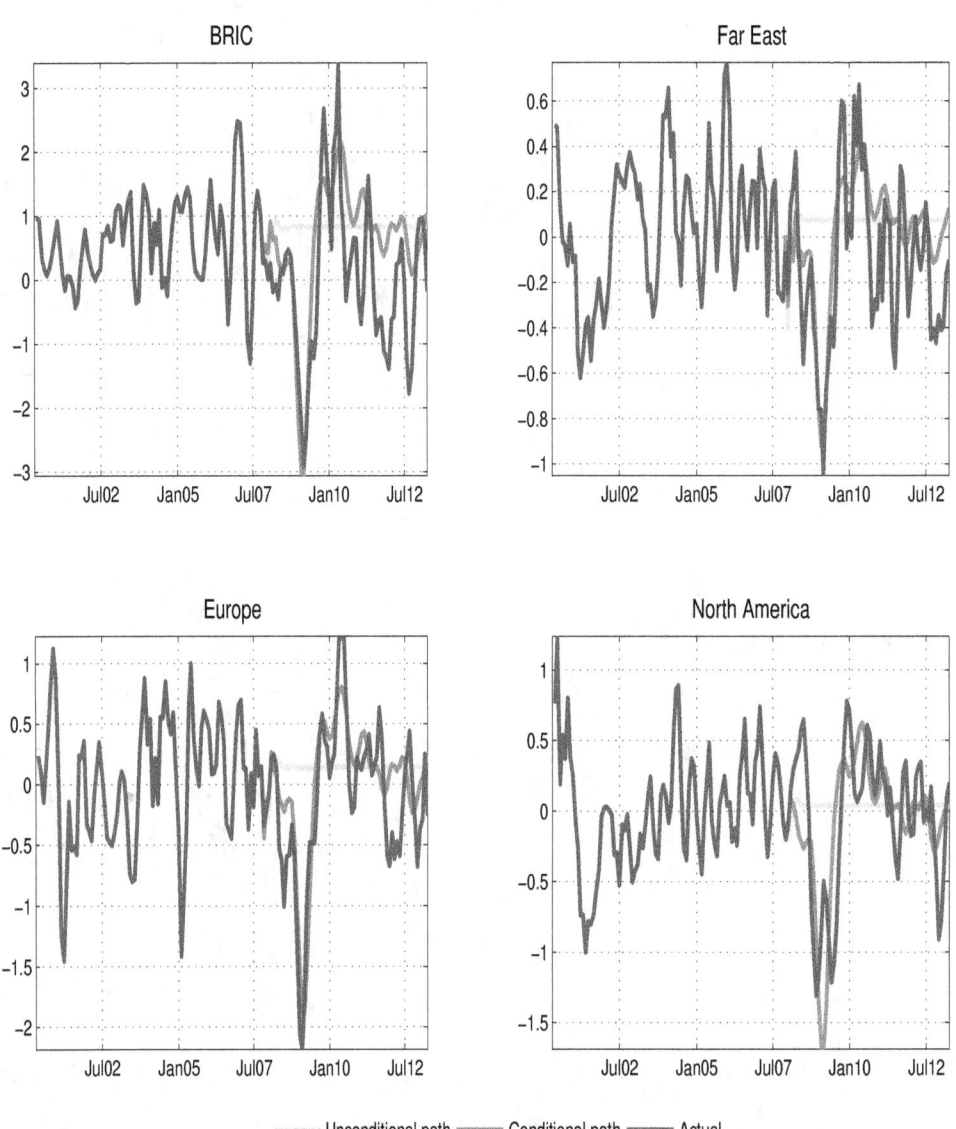

Note: Simulated extra euro area import volumes path over the sample November 2007 to April 2013; trade dynamics are conditional to the realized macro values from November 2007 to April 2013 and to the parameters estimated with the data available at the end of December 2007. The four sub-plots refer to different geographical areas. Values are in three-month-on-three-month (3Mo3M) growth rates.

Figure 12: Conditional path for export and import volumes - Rest of the World

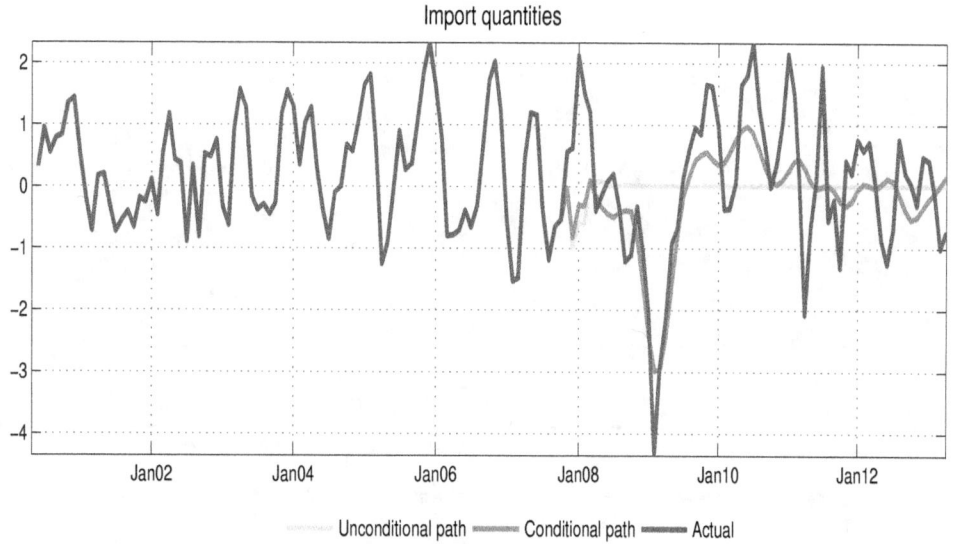

Unconditional path ——— Conditional path ——— Actual

Note: Simulated extra euro area export and import volumes paths over the sample November 2007 to April 2013; trade dynamics are conditional on the realized macro values from November 2007 to April 2013 and on the parameters estimated with the data available at the end of December 2007. The two sub-plots refer to exports and imports from the Rest of the World. Values are in three-month-on-three-month (3Mo3M) growth rates.

Figure 13: Generalized impulse response function for extra euro area export volumes

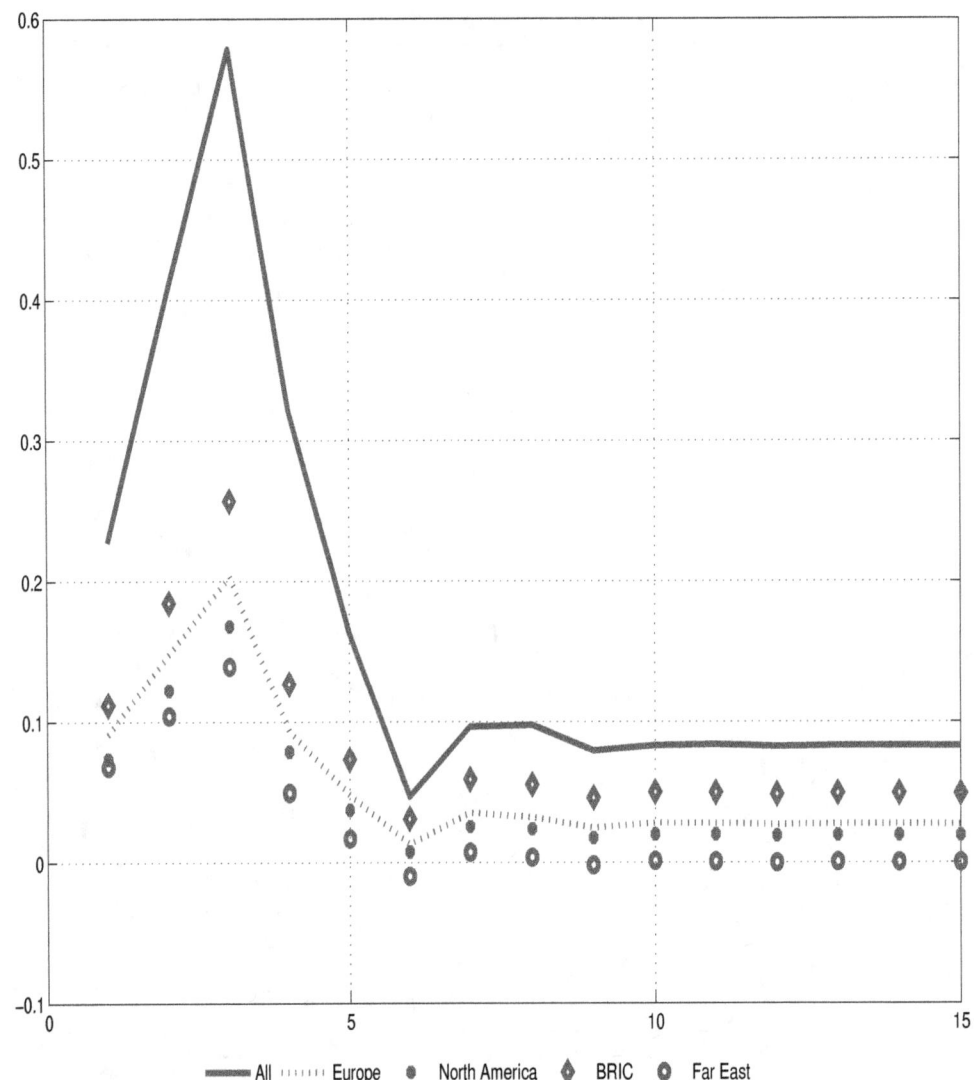

Note: All (blue, straight line) refers to the deviation of the conditional forecasts of extra euro area export volumes from the baseline, unconditional forecast. The conditional predictions are computed, first by multiplying the unconditional path of the external demand components (industrial production and purchasing manager index series) by 1.05 and then by computing predictions of the extra euro area series conditional on this scenario. A similar computation is done for the geographical breakdown (Europe, North America, BRIC, and Far East). The conditional forecasts for each single area are computed by multiplying by 1.05 the unconditional forecast of the external demand components of each specific area.

7 Appendix: Extra Tables

Table 3: Loadings Restrictions on Macro Variables

	f^1	f^2	f^3	f^4
U.K. PMI	1	0	0	0
India PMI	1	0	0	0
Japan PMI	1	0	0	0
Korea PMI	1	0	0	0
Russia PMI	1	0	0	0
Turkey PMI	1	0	0	0
U.S. PMI	1	0	0	0
Brazil IP	1	0	0	0
Canada IP	1	0	0	0
U.K. IP	1	0	0	0
India IP	1	0	0	0
Japan IP	1	0	0	0
Korea IP	1	0	0	0
Russia IP	1	0	0	0
Sweden IP	1	0	0	0
Turkey IP	1	0	0	0
US IP	1	0	0	0
Brazil PPI	0	0	0	1
Canada PPI	0	0	0	1
Denmark PPI	0	0	0	1
India PPI	0	0	0	1
Japan PPI	0	0	0	1
Sweden PPI	0	0	0	1
U.S. PPI	0	0	0	1
euro area IP	0	1	0	0
euro area RS	0	1	0	0
euro area UR	0	1	0	0
euro area REER	1	1	1	1
euro area CPI	0	0	1	0
euro area PPI	0	0	1	0

Note: Factor loadings structure on macro variables. PMI stands for purchasing manager index, IP for industrial production, PPI for producer price index, RS for retail sales, UR for unemployment rate, REER for real effective exchange rate and CPI for consumer price index. 1 indicates that there are no restrictions, 0 that the loading is restricted to zero.

Table 4: Loading Restrictions for the Model with only Trade Variables

	Export prices				Import prices				Export Volumes				Import Volumes			
	f^1	f^2	f^3	f^4	f^1	f^2	f^3	f^4	f^1	f^2	f^3	f^4	f^1	f^2	f^3	f^4
Brazil	0	0	1	0	0	0	0	1	0	1	0	0	0	1	0	0
Russia	0	0	1	0	0	0	0	1	0	1	0	0	0	1	0	0
India	0	0	1	0	0	0	0	1	0	1	0	0	0	1	0	0
Cina	0	0	1	0	0	0	0	1	0	1	1	0	0	1	0	0
Japan	0	0	1	0	0	0	0	1	0	1	0	0	0	1	0	0
Korea	0	0	1	0	0	0	0	1	0	1	0	0	0	1	0	0
Switzerland	0	0	1	0	0	0	0	1	0	1	0	0	0	1	0	0
Danimark	0	0	1	0	0	0	0	1	0	1	0	0	0	1	0	0
Sweden	0	0	1	0	0	0	0	1	0	1	0	0	0	1	0	0
UK	0	0	1	0	0	0	0	1	0	1	0	0	0	1	0	0
Turkey	0	0	1	0	0	0	0	1	0	1	0	0	0	1	0	0
US	0	0	1	0	0	0	0	1	0	1	1	0	0	1	0	0
Canada	0	0	1	0	0	0	0	1	0	1	0	0	0	1	0	0
OPEC	0	0	1	0	0	0	0	1	0	1	0	0	0	1	0	0
Extra	0	0	1	0	0	0	0	1	0	1	0	0	0	1	0	0
Intra	0	0	1	0	0	0	0	1	0	1	0	0	0	1	0	0
Rest of the World	0	0	1	0	0	0	0	1	0	1	0	0	0	1	0	0

Note: Factor loadings structure, 1 indicates that there are no restrictions, 0 that the loading is restricted to zero.